Little Bits of Whimsy:

A Pattern Book

by Kathleen
Rindal Brooks

CHITRA PUBLICATIONS

Your Best Value in Quilting

All Rights Reserved. Published in the United States of America.
Printed in Hong Kong.

Chitra Publications
2 Public Avenue
Montrose, Pennsylvania 18801-1220

First Printing: 1997

Library of Congress Cataloging-in-Publication Data

Brooks, Kathleen Rindal, 1956-
    Little bits of whimsy : a pattern book / by Kathleen Rindal
Brooks.
        p.   cm.
    ISBN 1-885588-15-1
    1. Quilting--Patterns.   2. Patchwork--Patterns.   3. Appliqué-
-Patterns.   4. Miniature quilts.   I. Title.
    TT835.B725 1997
    746.46'041--DC21   97-22066
                                                                    CIP

Edited by: Debra Feece
Design and Illustrations: Diane M. Albeck-Grick
Cover Photography: Guy Cali Associates, Inc., Clarks Summit, Pennsylvania;
Author's photo by Bridget Rowley, Chicago, Illinois
Inside Photography: Craige's Photography, Montrose, Pennsylvania;
Jim Newberry, Chicago, Illinois

Our Mission Statement:

*We publish quality quilting magazines and books
that recognize, promote and inspire self-expression.
We are dedicated to serving our customers
with respect, kindness and efficiency.*

Table of Contents

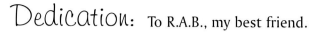

Dedication: To R.A.B., my best friend.

Introduction

When I saw my first miniature quilt with all those minuscule pieces, it was love at first sight! So I followed the pattern for a tiny schoolhouse, laboring over the 1/8" seams. A few weeks later my first miniature quilt was complete—but more than a little bit lopsided. Discouraged but determined, I began another. That was 1982. Since then I've made more than 70 miniature quilts.

Whenever I'm "on the road" lecturing about the great rewards of quilting on a small scale, I'm inundated with questions: How do I keep the sewing machine from chewing up my little patches? How do I get those perfect points to match? How do I quilt such tiny stitches? So began this book.

Practice is the greatest teacher. It's taught me that I don't ever need to struggle using big-quilt techniques for small-sized patchwork. Since miniature quilts are not just full-sized quilts made smaller, most design elements must be adjusted to fit the change in scale. Over the years I've discovered many short-cuts and specific precision techniques that ensure the accuracy crucial to a successful mini.

Here you will find some of my favorite tricks to make your little quilts "sing." From initial fabric selections to the very last stitch, these are tips that will save you lots of time and frustration. Whether you decide to use the patterns in this book or to apply my techniques to your original creations, enliven your next quilt with little bits of whimsy!

Kathleen

"May the favor of the Lord our God rest upon us; establish the work of our hands for us—yes, establish the work of our hands." Psalm 90:17

General Techniques

Fabric

I love quilts that are a little unpredictable. That means being open to uncertainty. If this idea makes you a bit nervous, it's okay. The risks you take with a miniature quilt are, by definition, small risks. You can afford to step out of your comfort zone.

The key to a successful miniature quilt is to do more in a smaller area. Since you have only tiny pieces of fabric to work with, the colors you choose should be more intense and have greater contrast than the colors you would use for a full-size quilt. It is often difficult to visualize how a postage stamp size piece of fabric will look surrounded by equally tiny pieces. To get a clearer idea of how a fabric will look in use, rough cut a small scrap about the size of the finished patch.

To create and intensify contrast in your work, stretch the palette by using a variety of fabrics in one color family rather than just different values of a single color. For example, a quilt made with blues that range from blue greens to royals to purple blues will be much more exciting than one with shades of gray blue. Taking this bold step can be difficult because it may initially appear that such different blues do not go together. However, because the furthest patches in your quilt may be only 10" apart, fabrics of like color tend to "connect" across the surface of the quilt. The clash of more unlikely combinations will add energy to your quilt. This is the reason I tend to use a wide variety of scraps, rarely repeating a fabric in my patchwork. Also, when selecting fabric for the borders and binding, I always choose fabrics that were not used elsewhere in that miniature.

Piecing with a variety of prints will create a wonderful texture on the surface of your quilt. Choose fabric of different patterns: leaves, vines, flowers, geometrics, dots, plaids, checks and stripes. Without this mixture, a quilt can appear flat and lifeless. Avoid fabrics where the design and background have the same scale; these will give your quilt a "busy" look. Fabrics with subtle prints are the most suitable. Two-color prints are also generally easier to use than multicolor ones. But, don't assume only small prints work well. Often a large print, where only a portion of the design will appear in your block, can be effective.

Specialty fabrics contribute depth and interest to your quilt in several ways. They can create a focal point. I love to use conversation prints (fabrics printed with small objects or images) in my work. Prepare paper windows the size and shape of the patches, then lay a window over your fabric to help visualize how that motif will look once it is pieced into the quilt. (See page 12.) Variegated fabrics, ones that shade from light to dark, provide light sources in your patchwork. Because you are working in miniature, however, you must be sure to cut the patch from an area of fabric where both the light and dark areas are represented. To add movement and a folksy quality to your quilt, use plaids and stripes cut slightly off grain.

Collecting fabrics is a favorite pastime of most quilters. If you're concerned that making miniatures will curtail expanding your "stash," not to worry. Miniatures, in fact, make great use of odd fabrics that you may never have imagined using before!

Use samples sent by fabric clubs and mail-order sources—a little piece can go a long way. When you attend classes and workshops, be the first one to clean up but the last one to leave. I've been known to glean scraps from the carpeting and even rummage through wastebaskets at the end of the day.

As you build your collection, be sure to periodically assess your fabrics in an organized way. Go through the color wheel and see if you have a range of fabrics in every area. To fill in the gaps, buy (or mooch) what you need, not just what you like.

Tools

The proper tools make any job simpler and there are endless gadgets on the market to make your quilting easier. Here are a few of my favorite "helpers":

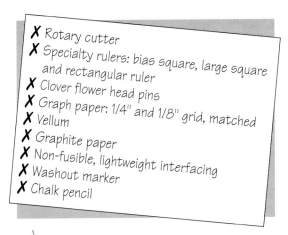

✗ Rotary cutter
✗ Specialty rulers: bias square, large square and rectangular ruler
✗ Clover flower head pins
✗ Graph paper: 1/4" and 1/8" grid, matched
✗ Vellum
✗ Graphite paper
✗ Non-fusible, lightweight interfacing
✗ Washout marker
✗ Chalk pencil

Designing

Viewing your design from a distance helps you make sound color decisions. A design wall is invaluable for this step of the process. Since small quilts do not require much layout space, you can easily rig a design "wall" for your miniatures. Just insert a sturdy piece of cardboard into a flannel pillowcase (or make a flannel "pocket" by sewing a folded piece of flannel on two sides, leaving one side open to insert the cardboard). Securing a piece of low-loft batting on a child's easel is another way to fashion a portable design wall.

Lay out the fabrics on your design surface the way you plan to sew them together. Then step back. If one of your choices doesn't seem to work, cut an alternate patch and try it instead. Even when I know red is the color I want in a particular position, I may audition 20 different reds in a broad spectrum of shades, tints and textures before I settle on the final choice. When you find the one that makes your quilt "sing," you've "met your patch."

Techniques

One of the first snags commonly encountered while piecing miniatures results from the sewing machine feed dogs "chewing up" the edges of tiny fabric patches. A simple trick for "taming the wild feed dogs" is to run a scrap of fabric through the machine ahead of the first patches to be seamed. Do not cut the thread between the scrap fabric and the patchwork. Beginning with a scrap keeps the edges of subsequent pieces from sliding into the throat plate opening and thereby prevents the feed dogs from fraying fabric edges. This chain piecing can be continued by feeding through the remaining pairs of patches, one after another.

I'd like to make a comment or two about the ever unpopular subject of ripping. The hard truth is, having to rip out stitches is an unavoidable reality for miniature quiltmakers. No matter how careful the stitcher or how accurate the workmanship, small pieces occasionally slip out of place. I always keep a seam ripper handy. If the points don't meet or the seams don't match, rip it out! Don't try to pull out the stitches by tugging on the bobbin thread; this may stretch or tear small pieces. Rip your stitches out carefully, one stitch at a time. The time you will otherwise spend compensating, stretching, easing and weeping will far exceed the 20 or 30 seconds necessary to just rip it out. While this may be a matter of attitude more than specific technique, a willingness to rip out and redo when necessary—perhaps more than any other "construction" technique—can make the difference between a wonder of precision and a kittywampus nice try. Your quilt may be around for generations. The extra effort will show and be admired for years to come.

Anytime you're working with small pieces, traditional piecing methods can be quite frustrating. Depending on which kind of block I'm creating, there are a couple of ways I circumvent this struggle. Generally I resort to either "cutting down" or to foundation piecing. Each method maximizes accuracy in its own way, allowing you to work with larger patches of fabric and then reduce them to miniature proportions.

Downsizing

Although it only works for a limited number of simple blocks, cutting down is the simplest technique for downsizing patchwork. Use it for Pinwheel blocks, Four Patch blocks, bias squares or any other block where the "action" takes place in the center of the block and grows outward as the block size increases.

When two small patches need to be joined, I cut my fabric as if for a larger block and sew the pieces together with a 1/4" seam. Press the seams to one side, then trim the seams to 1/8" and rotary cut the block to size. For example, if my quilt requires a 1" Four Patch block, I make a 3" Four Patch block, and then cut it down to the required 1" size.

Foundation Piecing

My favorite construction method is foundation piecing. Many of the quilts in this book utilize this simple and accurate technique.

When making one of these quilts, begin by photocoping or tracing the foundation pattern onto lightweight paper. I prefer vellum, a translucent drafting paper (available at art or drafting supply stores). The ability to see the pattern from both sides of the paper will take the guesswork out of where to place your fabric. I do not recommend copying onto tracing paper because it is not durable enough to withstand the ripping out of stitches, should that be necessary. An additional benefit, and the primary reason why I use vellum almost exclusively is that it tears away easily and cleanly when piecing is complete.

Since the ability to see your drawing on both sides of the paper is helpful, you can use graphite paper (if your photocopied or traced pattern is not on vellum) to transfer the design to the reverse side of the paper. Although similar to carbon paper, graphite does not rub off on fingers or fabric. Place the graphite paper, right side up, against the back of the pattern. Then trace over the pattern using a mechanical pencil with the lead removed. The pattern will be transferred to the back without the sewing lines on the front being blurred by pencil marks. It's okay if this tracing is a bit imprecise since your sewing will follow the photocopied pattern. These traced lines simply help you place your fabrics accurately.

Once your paper pattern is ready, the sewing can finally begin. In preparation, thread your sewing machine with a neutral (gray or beige) color thread. Set the stitch length at 15-20 stitches per inch (or at 2.0 on a European machine); a short stitch length perforates the paper often enough to enable you to tear it away more easily later. Do not be tempted to set the stitch length too short or you risk the paper detaching too soon.

To begin the actual piecing, locate the first piece (#1) on your paper pattern, then rough cut a scrap of fabric at least 1/4" larger on all sides than the size of that area. Lay the fabric patch, right side up, covering section #1. Rough cut a second scrap of fabric large enough to cover area #2 and extend beyond it at least 1/4" on all sides. Place this piece right side up, covering pattern area #2. Check its placement before flipping piece #2 right side down. Secure both pieces with a pin. Turn the entire unit over and sew along the pattern line between #1 and #2, beginning and ending just a few stitches beyond each end of the line. Clip the threads and trim the seam allowance to 1/8", taking care not to cut the foundation. Press the fabrics open. Continue adding pieces in numerical sequence, remembering to trim the seam allowances and press as you go, until your block is complete. Baste around the edges of the block within the 1/4" seam allowance. Now correct your block size by trimming it to the size of the finished block plus a 1/4" seam allowance on each side. NOTE: Favorite Foundation Pieced Minis, *also published by Chitra Publications, provides Step-by-Step photos describing this technique.*

Once all your blocks are complete, you are ready to assemble the quilt top. Sew the blocks into rows, pressing seams of adjacent rows in opposite directions. Pin the finished rows, snugly butting intersecting seams together. And now, the tip that will save you hours of ripping time on your little (or even big) quilts—sew only at each intersecting seam (not from the beginning to the end of the row) in the following way: Take just five or six stitches through the first seam intersection, then stop! Lift the presser foot and scoot to the next intersecting seam, and repeat the "take-five-or-six-stitches; then-stop-again" process. Once all the intersecting seams are anchored this way, open the rows and scrutinize the seams carefully. If they match up precisely, great. If not, rip that one intersection carefully and try again. When all the seams are properly aligned, you can safely stitch the rows together from beginning to end.

Once all the rows have been joined, add borders (if any), and give the quilt top its final pressing.

Now comes the step everybody dislikes—removing all the paper. At this stage, it is helpful to remember all the time and frustration that foundation piecing has saved you—because this is where you may be paying for it! (If you used vellum, here's where that bit of extra cash you spent will save you big time!) Now plop yourself in front of the TV and carefully tear away the paper pieces one by one. Stubborn fragments can be coaxed free after a light misting of water with a spray bottle. Do not re-press your quilt once the paper has been removed or you risk hopelessly distorting all your perfect piecing.

Quilting Design

For many quilters, one of the most appealing features of a small quilt is the relatively short amount of time required to complete the actual quilting.

Since my least favorite part of the entire process is marking the quilting design, I often make use of existing lines on the quilt. Quilting "in the ditch" is the simplest way to determine quilting lines. For my borders, I often choose fabrics with straight lines or swirls that I can follow with my stitch. Freehand quilting designs—loose cables, squiggles or random meandering are all favorites of mine.

I often quilt dates and messages into the borders of my quilts. Write a message in large cursive lettering or big bubble letters. Stretch your handwriting to fill a larger space; stagger the lettering up and down to squeeze in more.

Sometimes traditional quilts require a more formal quilting pattern, especially in the border. Cables, fans and zigzags require measuring and marking. Commercial templates are available in all sizes but rarely does the length fit perfectly enough to complete the corners smoothly. To remedy this, I take a piece of non-fusible lightweight interfacing and cut it to the exact size of my borders, with corners included; this will resemble a picture frame of interfacing with the center cut out. Using a washout marker, I then proceed to mark the interfacing as if it were the actual quilt border. It is here that I practice stretching or squeezing the border design and reconciling the corners. Some designs will need just a bit of "fudging" while others may require a complete makeover. Mark the design all the way around the interfacing prototype—no quilting halfway! Only then will you be sure that your design will fit precisely without any later need for re-marking your quilt top, which often stretches your border fabric and causes it to ripple. After you have drawn the full border design on the interfacing, you are ready to transfer it to your quilt top.

Following the interfacing mock-up as a guide, mark the actual quilt top. The original commercial quilting templates can usually be used directly, making any necessary spacing adjustments as you go. If this seems too complicated, make a new template from your interfacing: simply use scissors to cut a channel along your custom designed quilting lines, lay the interfacing on top of the border and mark as usual. I mark very lightly with a chalk pencil on dark fabrics. On a light-colored border, I often use a fine-tip washable marker. Whatever method of marking you choose, it is essential that your marks can be easily and completely removed. Miniature quilts are viewed more closely and any telltale transfer lines will be noticeable!

Batting

If your miniatures look more like hotpads than little quilts, it probably means your batting is too thick. Since even a low-loft batting is often too thick when working in this scale, I split a low-loft or cotton batt. Cut the batting about an inch larger than the size of the quilt top. Beginning at one corner, carefully peel the layers apart. The fibers may be a little difficult to separate at first but a bit of patience does the trick. Move your hands as you go, keeping your fingers near the spot where the batt is being halved. Pull the fibers apart slowly, smoothing down any loose ones.

Once the batting is split in two, lay the smooth side of one piece against the wrong side of the quilt top. Save the other piece for your next quilt. I do not recommend using flannel in place of batting. Insufficient loft results in a finished look that is too flat, causing your quilting stitch to look more like an embroidered running stitch.

Backing

Since miniature quilts offer so little opportunity for using big chunks of favorite fabrics, take advantage of your quilt back as a spot to splash that yardage you've been longing to use. Choose something exciting or fun, perhaps a larger scale conversation print that plays off the front of the quilt.

If you are a beginner at hand-quilting, use a highly patterned fabric that will hide any poor quilting stitches or ones which may not come all the way through to the backing.

Basting

Layer the backing, batting and quilt top; then baste the layers together in a grid pattern with stitching lines about an inch apart. A well-basted quilt will not shift during the quilting process, and it is this that produces a flat finished product. I have not found either pin basting or the new plastic basting fasteners to be adequate for miniatures as they do not hold the layers together securely enough.

Although it is natural to want to move quickly on to the quilting, do not skimp at this basting stage. Care during this step will guarantee that your little fabrication remains flat and square.

Binding

If you have basted well, it's not necessary to quilt your miniature before binding. In fact, I prefer to bind the quilt first, then go back and quilt it. I bind each side individually—consequently, there are no mitered corners.

Measure the vertical length of the quilt across the middle, not along the edge. From the lengthwise or crosswise grain of the binding fabric, cut a 1 1/8" wide strip equal to the quilt's longer sides. Then lay this binding right side down on the long edge of the layered, basted top. Sew with a scant 1/4" seam (no more!), stitching from top edge to bottom edge. Trim away excess batting and backing. Next, open up the binding and gently press it flat, being careful not to flatten the batting with the iron.

Now turn the quilt over so the back is facing up. Fold the binding over until the raw edge of the binding lays against the raw edge of the quilt back—then press lightly with your iron. Fold this pressed edge over until it meets the stitching line, then blindstitch into place. Repeat this process for the opposite edge.

Measure the horizontal width across the middle of the quilt. Cut a strip of binding equal to the width plus 1/2". On each end of this binding strip, press 1/4" to the wrong side of the binding. Maintaining these folds, sew the bindings to both remaining sides of the quilt. Trim away excess batting and backing. Fold the binding up and over and press as before. To form neat, square corners, blindstitch the binding corners closed. If it's not neat and square, rip out the machine stitching, refold the end, then restitch. This step can be a bit tedious, but proper alignment is a visible detail which will affect the overall appearance of your quilt. After the corners are complete, blindstitch the binding edge in place.

Quilting

If you have basted well, there is no need to use a quilting hoop. I prefer quilting without a hoop to ensure the quilt top remains undistorted as I stitch.

I use a leather thimble and a small needle, generally a #12 between. Use the smallest needle you can easily handle. Small stitches are, of course, mainly a result of practice, but a fine needle and no hoop can really help a lot. In addition, I often quilt my miniatures with regular sewing thread rather than a coated quilting thread. Not only does this give you a larger color range from which to choose, but the thinness of the thread actually makes your stitches appear smaller. Sewing thread, however, is not as strong as quilting thread, so you must use a shorter length—no more than 12" of thread. If the thread begins to fray, tie it off and resume quilting with a new piece.

It is usually the first stitch you take that is the most difficult to keep straight and small, so pay close attention to your needle placement. On a straightaway, I load my needle with as many stitches as it will hold before pulling the thread.

If you are unhappy with your quilting stitch, use a thread color without much contrast and stitch in the ditch.

Display your best stitches where others are most likely to look closely—around the borders and in other open areas!

Hanging Your Quilt

I hang my quilts with strips of Velcro®. Whipstitch a length of the soft loop part of non-adhesive Velcro along the top edge of the quilt back. Using small brads about an inch apart, nail the corresponding hook side length to the wall. The quilt can then be removed easily from the wall and exchanged with another of similar size.

Shown on page 17

Intermediate

A Chicken in Every Pot

Stitch your own neighborhood with this versatile pattern.

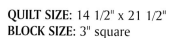

QUILT SIZE: 14 1/2" x 21 1/2"
BLOCK SIZE: 3" square

MATERIALS

Yardage is estimated for 44" fabric.
- 2" x 6" scrap for each of 15 houses
- 1 1/2" x 2" coordinating scrap for each gable
- 1 1/2" x 20" strip, red for the doors
- 1/8 yard blue for the roofs
- 1" x 36" strip, brick print for the chimneys
- 3/4" x 15" strip, small plaid for the windows
- 1/4 yard one light print fabric or scraps totaling 1/4 yard for the sky
- 1/8 yard green for the grass
- 1/4 yard tiny black and white check for the sashing strips
- Piece of fabric with 24 printed motifs, each one no larger than 1/2" for the cornerstones
- 1/4 yard blue for the border
- 1/8 yard binding fabric
- 17" x 24" piece of backing fabric
- 17" x 24" piece of thin batting
- Paper for foundations

CUTTING
- Cut 15: A, blue roof fabric
- Cut 15: B, gable scraps
- Cut 15: C, chimney fabric
- Cut 15: C, light print sky fabric
- Cut 38: 1" x 3 1/2" strips, sashing fabric
- Cut 24: 1" squares, with one printed motif centered in each square for the cornerstones NOTE: *For ease in centering the motif in each square, see "You can do Windows" on page 15.*

PIECING
Follow the Foundation Piecing *instructions*

in General Techniques *to make the foundations and to piece the blocks. Make 15 foundations from pattern A and 15 from pattern B.*

For foundation A:
- Use the following fabrics in these positions:
    1 - window fabric
    2, 3, 4, 5 - house scrap
    6 - red door fabric
    7 - house scrap
    8 - grass fabric
    9 - Join a blue roof A to a gable B to form a roof unit, as shown in the diagram.

Sew it to the foundation as section 9.
    10, 11 - sky fabric

For foundation B:
- Use the following fabrics in these positions:
    1 - chimney fabric
    2, 3, 4 - sky fabric
    5 - Join a chimney fabric C and a sky fabric C to form a chimney unit and sew

it to the foundation as section 5.
    6 - sky fabric
- Baste each foundation in the seam allowance and trim on the broken line.
- Join a house foundation and a roof foundation to complete a block. Make 15.

ASSEMBLY
- Lay out 3 houses in a row.
- Sew 1" x 3 1/2" sashing strips between the house blocks and on each end of the row. Press all seams in the same direction. Make 5 rows.
- Make a sashing row by alternating four cornerstones and three sashing strips, beginning and ending with a cornerstone. Press all seams in the opposite direction from those in the house rows. Make 6.
- Sew the sashing rows between the house rows. Sew one sashing row to the top of the quilt and one to the bottom.

BORDERS
- Measure the length of the patchwork. Cut 2 blue borders 2" wide by that length. Sew the borders to the long sides of the patchwork.

- Measure the width of the patchwork (including borders). Cut 2 blue borders 2" wide by that width. Sew the borders to the remaining sides of the patchwork.
- Press the quilt top and remove the paper foundations.

FINISHING
- Layer the quilt top, batting and backing. Baste. Bind the edges following the instructions in *General Techniques*.

Full-Size Border Quilting Design for A Chicken in Every Pot and Country Living

Full-Size Foundation Patterns for A Chicken in Every Pot

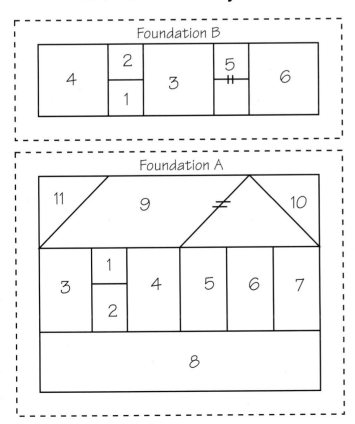

Full-Size Template Patterns for A Chicken in Every Pot

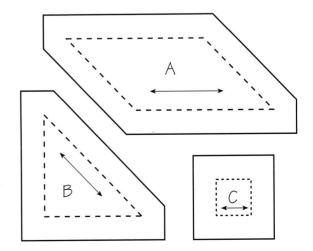

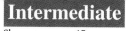

Hole in the Barn Door

Turn your imagination and your bag of scraps loose!

QUILT SIZE: 8" x 10"
BLOCK SIZE: 1 7/8" square

MATERIALS
Yardage is estimated for 44" fabric.
- 12 dark scraps at least 3" x 5 1/2" each
- 1/8 yard tan
- 1/8 yard blue check for the border
- 1/8 yard red print for the binding
- 10" x 12" piece of backing fabric
- 10" x 12" piece of thin batting

CUTTING
- Cut 24: 2" squares, 2 from each dark scrap
- Cut 12: 1" x 5" strips, 1 from each dark scrap
- Cut 24: 2" squares, tan
- Cut 12: 1" x 5" strips, tan
- Cut 12: 1 1/8" squares, tan

PIECING
- Layer one 2" dark square and one 2" tan square right sides together. Draw a diagonal line from corner to corner on the tan square. Stitch 1/4" to the right and left of this line. Cut along the pencil line. Open the squares and press the seams toward the dark fabric. Using a bias square ruler, trim the squares to 1 1/8". Repeat this procedure using the remaining 2" dark squares and 2" tan squares. You will have 12 sets of 4 matching bias squares.
- Sew a 1" x 5" dark strip and a 1" x 5" tan strip right sides together along their length. Press the seam allowance toward the dark fabric. Make 12.
- Cut four 1 1/8" pieces from each sewn strip.

ASSEMBLY
- Assemble the blocks as shown in the diagram. Make 12 blocks.

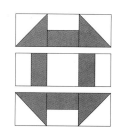

- Lay out 4 rows of 3 blocks.
- Sew the blocks together in rows. Press the seams of adjacent rows in opposite directions. Join the rows.
- Measure the length of the patchwork. Cut 2 blue check borders 1 1/2" wide by that length. Sew the borders to the long sides of the patchwork.
- Measure the width of the patchwork (including borders). Cut 2 blue check borders 1 1/2" wide by that width. Sew the borders to the top and bottom of the patchwork.

FINISHING
- Layer the quilt top, batting and backing. Baste. Bind the edges following the instructions in *General Techniques*.

QUILTING
- Quilt the blocks in the ditch. For the border, use the cable quilting design given on page 32.

OTHER IDEAS
- To add an amusing twist, center a tiny cow motif in each "hole" and use "moo" fabric for one of the patches.
- Use a variety of barn animals in the center of each block.
- Quilt the border in a fence design.

Brick Wall Charm

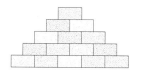

Simple cutting and piecing make this the perfect quilt for a beginner.

QUILT SIZE: 13 1/4" x 16 1/2"
BLOCK SIZE: 1" x 1 3/4"

MATERIALS
Yardage is estimated for 44" fabric.
- 66 scraps at least 1 1/2" x 2 1/4" each, all different for a charm quilt
- 1/4 yard fabric for the border
- 1/8 yard binding fabric
- 15 1/4" x 18 1/2" piece of backing fabric
- 15 1/4" x 18 1/2" piece of thin batting

CUTTING
Dimensions include a 1/4" seam allowance.
- Cut 66: 1 1/2" x 2 1/4" rectangles, assorted scraps

PIECING
- Lay out five 1 1/2" x 2 1/4" rectangles end to end. Sew them into a strip to form row A. Make 6.
- Lay out six 1 1/2" x 2 1/4" rectangles end to end. Sew them into a strip to form row B. Make 6.

ASSEMBLY
- Sew rows A and B together, staggering the seams so the seams in row B fall in the centers of the bricks in row A. (The ends of row B will extend past the ends of row A. Do not trim them off until the entire quilt top is pieced.)
- Continue adding rows to the previous unit, alternating rows A and B. Use row 1 as your guideline for lining up the seams.
- Use a rotary cutter and square ruler to trim the row B's even with the row A's

(continued on bottom of page 11)

Signature Quilt

Preserve your memories with a special keepsake.

QUILT SIZE: 9 1/2" x 12 1/2"
BLOCK SIZE: 2 1/4" square

MATERIALS
Yardage is estimated for 44" fabric.
- Assorted dark, medium and light print scraps totaling 1/4 yard
- 1/8 yard muslin for signatures
- 1/8 yard dark print for the border
- 1/8 yard binding fabric
- 11 1/2" x 14 1/2" piece of backing fabric
- 11 1/2" x 14 1/2" piece of thin batting
- Paper for foundations
- Black or brown fine tip Pigma pen

PIECING
Follow the Foundation Piecing *instructions in* General Techniques *to make the foundations and to piece the blocks. Make 7 foundations from pattern A and 10 from pattern B.*
For foundation A:
- Use the following fabrics in these positions:
   1, 2 - different medium prints
   3 - muslin
   4, 5, 6, 7 - one dark print
   8, 9, 10, 11 - one light or medium print
For foundation B:
- Use the following fabrics in these positions:
   1 - muslin
   2, 3 - one dark print
   4, 5, 6 - one light or medium print
- Baste each foundation in the seam allowance and trim on the broken line.

ASSEMBLY
- Referring to the photo, lay out the blocks "on point." Sew the blocks into diagonal rows. Join the rows.
- Measure the length of the patchwork. Cut 2 borders 1 3/4" wide by that length. Sew the borders to the sides of the patchwork.
- Measure the width of the patchwork (including borders). Cut 2 borders 1 3/4" wide by that width. Sew the borders to the top and bottom of the patchwork.

FINISHING
- Press the quilt top and remove the paper foundations.
- Layer the quilt top, batting and backing. Baste. Bind the edges following the instructions in *General Techniques*.

QUILTING
- For a unique effect use a quilting stencil intended for a full-size quilt. I used a Baptist Fan design to cover the surface of my miniature.

OTHER IDEAS
- Why not create a space for someone else to preserve her own memories? For a special birthday or anniversary celebration, make this quilt but leave the signature blocks blank; wrap the quilt, include a fabric pen and let the guests do the rest.
- For a fundraiser, raffle or auction make a fill-in-the-blank signature quilt and let the lucky recipient have one more way to make the quilt her very own.

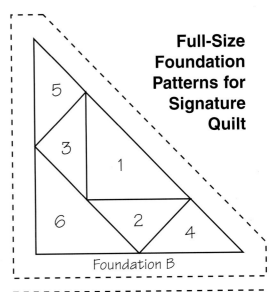

Full-Size Foundation Patterns for Signature Quilt

Foundation B

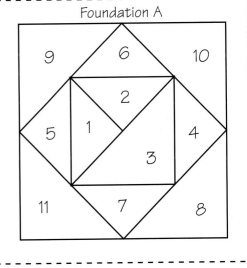

Foundation A

Brick Wall Charm continued
along the sides.
- Measure the length of the patchwork. Cut 2 borders 2 1/2" wide by that length. Sew the borders to the sides of the patchwork.
- Measure the width of the patchwork (including borders). Cut 2 borders 2 1/2" wide by that width. Sew the borders to the top and bottom of the patchwork.

FINISHING
- Layer the quilt top, batting and backing. Baste. Bind the edges following the instructions in *General Techniques*.

QUILTING
- Quilt in the ditch or across each block, corner to corner.
- Quilt a message in the border or try

the "ice cream cone" quilting design found on page 32. Quilt your initials and the date in a corner.

ANOTHER IDEA
- For a 16 1/2" x 20" doll quilt, cut 71 bricks 1 3/4" x 3". Follow the instructions, adding an additional row (13 rows).

Granny Wore Star Pajamas

Use vintage scraps for an old-fashioned look.

QUILT SIZE: 9 1/2" x 11 3/4"
BLOCK SIZE: 2 1/4" square

MATERIALS
Yardage is estimated for 44" fabric.
• 1/8 yard red solid fabric for the block centers and the narrow inner border
• Red print scrap at least 4" x 7"
• Red and white stripe at least 4" x 9"
• Red and white print at least 6" x 7"
• Red and white check at least 7" x 8"
• Blue print at least 7" x 8"
• 1/8 yard blue and white star print for the blocks and the binding
• 1/8 yard blue and white check for the blocks and the outer border
• 1/8 yard white or light print
• 12" x 14" piece of backing fabric
• 12" x 14" piece of thin batting
• Paper for foundations

CUTTING
• Cut 2: 1" x 9 1/2" strips, red, for the narrow inner border
• Cut 2: 1" x 8 1/4" strips, red, for the narrow inner border
• Cut 2: 2" x 10 1/2" strips, blue and white check, for the outer border
• Cut 2: 2" x 9 3/4" strips, blue and white check, for the outer border

PIECING
Follow the Foundation Piecing *instructions in* General Techniques *to make 12 foundations and to piece the blocks.*
For each block:
• Use the following fabrics in these positions:
    1 - red solid
    2, 3 - red print
    4, 5 - blue and white star print
    6, 7 - red and white stripe
    8, 9 - blue and white check
    10, 11 - red and white print
    12, 13 - blue print
    14, 15 - red and white check
    16, 17 - white or light print
• Baste each foundation in the seam allowance and trim on the broken line.

ASSEMBLY
• Lay out 4 rows of 3 blocks. Rotate the blocks so the lights and darks form a secondary pattern. In this case, diagonal stripes form "straight furrows."
• Sew the blocks into rows. Press the seams of adjacent rows in opposite directions. Join the rows.
• Sew the 1" x 9 1/2" red strips to the long sides of the quilt.
• Sew the 1" x 8 1/4" red strips to the remaining sides of the quilt.
• Using a 5/8" seam, sew the 2" x 10 1/2" borders to the sides of the patchwork. Using this large seam allowance makes the piecing more manageable. Check the 1/8" inner border for accuracy. Rip and readjust if necessary. Press the border and trim the seam allowance to 1/4".
• Using a 5/8" seam, sew the 2" x 9 3/4" borders to the top and bottom of the patchwork. Check the 1/8" inner border for accuracy. Rip and readjust if necessary. Press the border and trim the seam allowance to 1/4".

FINISHING
• Press the quilt top and remove the paper foundations.
• Layer the quilt top, batting and backing. Baste. Bind the edges following the instructions in *General Techniques*.

QUILTING
• Quilt in the ditch in concentric squares. Stitch along the inner border. Quilt short, parallel lines across the width of the outer border using the checks as a guide.

You can do Windows!

Use paper or cardboard "windows" to get an idea of how a novelty print will work to best advantage in your quilt.

Here's how:
• Make the outside dimensions of the window frame the size and shape of the pattern piece, including seam allowances.
• Make the inside dimensions the size and shape of the finished quilt piece.

• Place the window on the right side of your fabric and adjust as desired.
• When the fabric in the window appears as you would like it in the finished quilt, simply trace and cut around the outside edge.

Full-Size Foundation Pattern for Granny Wore Star Pajamas

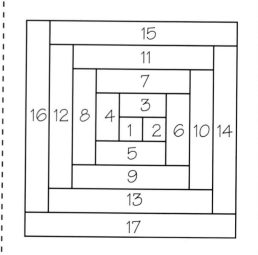

Quilt Gallery

▲ Your "dusty" country scraps will find a home in **"Hole in the Barn Door"** (8" x 10"). Add a checked border to complete the down-home look. The pattern is on page 10.

▲ I stitched **"Brick Wall Charm"** (13 1/4" x 16 1/2") in front of the television during the fall of the Berlin Wall. Its simple design looks as charming in brights or pastels as it does in dark prints. This traditional pattern is so easy to assemble, you'll want to make several! The pattern is on page 10.

◀ In **"House Medallion"** (9 3/4" square), two foundation-pieced borders accent the quaint cottage, also foundation pieced. There's even a narrow border where you can add a personal message. You can make this one with chimneys or without, it's charming either way! Wouldn't this make a perfect housewarming gift? The pattern is on page 23.

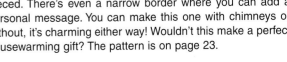

13

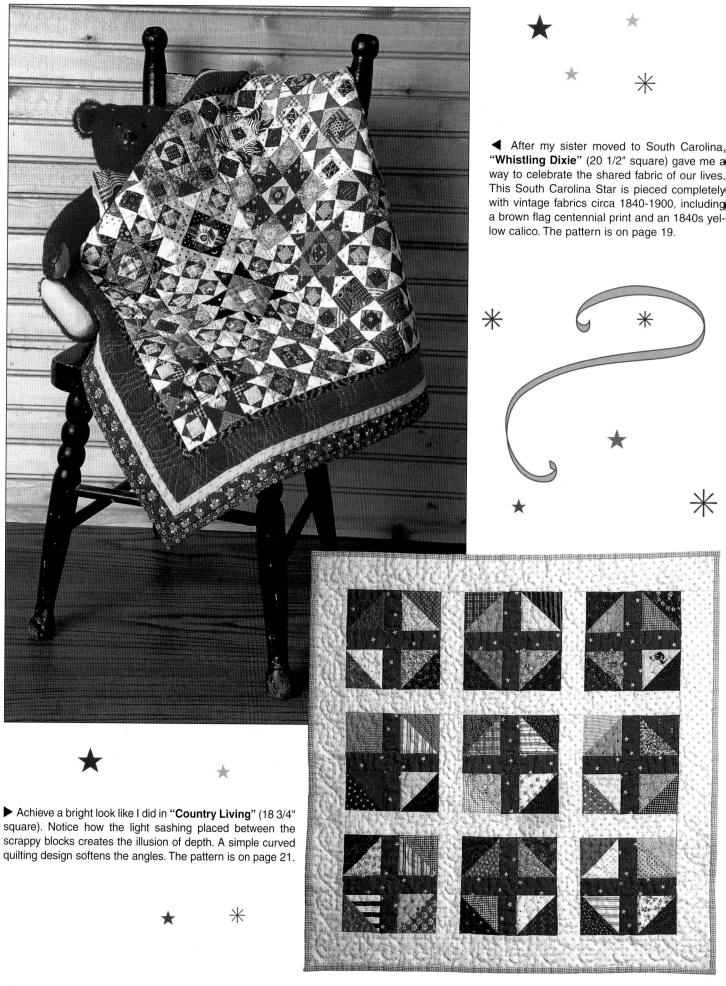

◀ After my sister moved to South Carolina, **"Whistling Dixie"** (20 1/2" square) gave me a way to celebrate the shared fabric of our lives. This South Carolina Star is pieced completely with vintage fabrics circa 1840-1900, including a brown flag centennial print and an 1840s yellow calico. The pattern is on page 19.

▶ Achieve a bright look like I did in **"Country Living"** (18 3/4" square). Notice how the light sashing placed between the scrappy blocks creates the illusion of depth. A simple curved quilting design softens the angles. The pattern is on page 21.

▶ I created **"Button Up"** (15" square) to show-case my collection of antique calico buttons. With or without buttons, it's fun to piece and delightful to own! The pattern is on page 26.

◀ Unusual motifs create a focal point in each block of **"Star Struck"** (16" x 19 3/4"). Though this one has a celebrity theme, yours could showcase Christmas motifs, animals, flowers—set your imagination free! The pattern is on page 31.

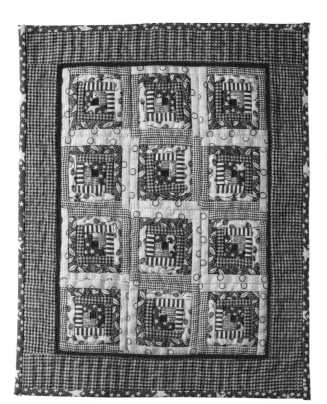

▲ Piece by piece, I pulled the fabrics for **"Granny Wore Star Pajamas"** (9 1/2" x 11 3/4") from my great-grandmother's scrap bag. One of the vintage prints is from an old pair of star print pj's! The pattern is on page 12.

▲ A **"Signature Quilt"** (9 1/2" x 12 1/2") can make memories of special occasions last long after the moment has passed. Make one for friends and relatives to sign at your next gathering. The pattern is on page 11.

◄ **"Pineapple Log Cabin Color Study"** (11" square) gives you a great excuse to collect more fabric! Each block repeats the same color scheme with different fabrics. The pattern is on page 29.

▶ "Charmeuse" (12" x 13 1/2") takes its name from the French word meaning "Little Charmer." This charm quilt contains 336 different prints. Over a dozen conversation prints within the patchwork create a visual hide and seek. The pattern is on page 20.

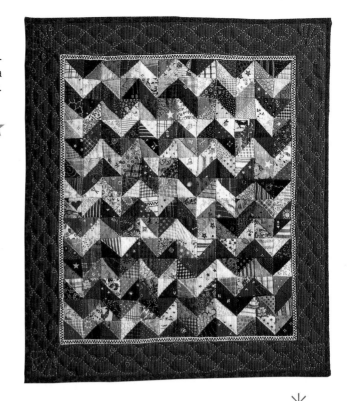

▲ Dig through your scrap pile and pick out your favorite prints for "Tumbler Charm" (13 3/4" x 17"). This "charming" miniature has 99 different fabrics. It's a cinch to piece so be sure to make more than one—everybody will want yours! The pattern is on page 22.

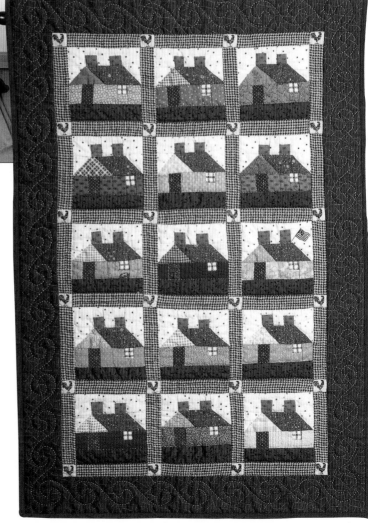

▶ The fabrics used in "A Chicken in Every Pot" (14 1/2" x 21 1/2") are like colorful personalities! Many different scraps add variety while the repeated use of one conversation print creates continuity. The pattern is on page 8.

17

◀ **"My Favorite Things"** (4 3/4" square, upper right, pattern on page 32) is an adorable mini that uses conversation prints for interest. Vintage fabrics and conversation prints lend a folk art quality to **"Puss in the Corner"** (6" square, left, pattern on page 28). Wear your heart on a quilt by making **"Sweethearts"** (3 3/4" x 4 1/4", lower right, pattern on page 28). Surprise yourself with a technique that only looks complex.

▶ One of life's simplest pleasures is sharing tea or coffee with someone you're close to. **"Teacups"** (13" x 15 1/2") is the perfect gift for that special person in your life. The pattern is on page 30.

Whistling Dixie

Make a bold statement by repeating just two small blocks.

QUILT SIZE: 20 1/2" square
BLOCK SIZE: 3 3/4" square

MATERIALS

Yardage is estimated for 44" fabric.
- Light, medium and dark print scraps (include blue, red, green, gold, pink, navy, black, tan and brown)
- 1/8 yard brown print for the first border
- 1/4 yard red print for the second border
- 1/8 yard yellow print for third border
- 1/4 yard navy print for fourth border
- 1/8 yard binding fabric
- 22 1/2" square of backing fabric
- 22 1/2" square of thin batting
- Paper for foundations

HINT

- To add interest, create a variety of tones within a block by substituting similar fabric for its counterpart within the block. For example, replace the original navy print with a different navy print in one section of the block only. A print of similar color and texture will add a bit of novelty, while a completely unexpected choice (substituting a green for a red, for instance), will give your quilt a whimsical flair. (It also offers an excuse to acquire more fabric!)

PIECING

Follow the Foundation Piecing *instructions in* General Techniques *to make the foundations and to piece the blocks. Make 80 foundations from pattern A and 64 from pattern B.*
For each of 16 blocks:
NOTE: *Each block will be made from 5 foundation A's and 4 foundation B's. One foundation A will be the center of the block, while the other 4 are the corner units. Make 4 identical corner units. Use different scraps for the center block. Follow the piecing order below to complete the A and B units.*
For foundation A:
- Use the following fabrics in these positions:
   1 - dark or medium print
   2, 3, 4, 5 - one dark or medium print
   6, 7, 8, 9 - one light or medium print
NOTE: *Piece 4 matching units of foundation*

B for each block. While there is little technical advantage to sewing block B on paper, the paper helps stabilize the fabric and ensures accurate results.
For foundation B:
- Use the following fabrics in these positions:
   1 - light print
   2 - medium print
   3 - Join a dark print A and a medium print A (the same print used in position 2) to make one unit, as shown. Sew the unit to the foundation in position 3.
- Baste each foundation in the seam allowance and trim on the broken line.

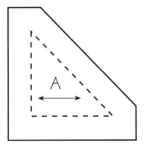

ASSEMBLY

- Refer to the diagram to construct the block. Make 16 blocks.

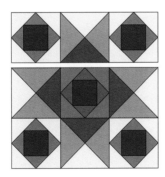

- Arrange the blocks in 4 rows of 4. Sew the blocks into rows.
- Press the seams of adjacent rows in opposite directions. Join the rows.
- Measure the length of the patchwork. Cut 2 brown borders 3/4" wide by that length. Sew them to opposite sides of the patchwork.
- Measure the width of the patchwork (including borders). Cut 2 brown borders 3/4" wide by that width. Sew them to the remaining sides of the patchwork.
- Measure and cut four 1 3/4" wide red borders in the same manner. Sew the borders to the edges of the patchwork.
- Measure and cut four 7/8" wide yellow borders in the same manner. Sew the borders to the edges of the patchwork.
- Measure and cut four 1 3/8" wide navy

borders in the same manner. Sew the borders to the edges of the patchwork.

FINISHING

- Press the quilt top and remove the paper foundations.
- Layer the quilt top, batting and backing. Baste. Bind the edges following the instructions in *General Techniques*.

QUILTING

- Quilt the blocks in the ditch.

Full-Size Template Pattern for Whistling Dixie

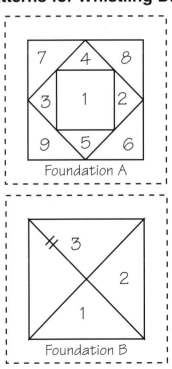

Full-Size Foundation Patterns for Whistling Dixie

Foundation A

Foundation B

Charmeuse

Stitch a "Little Charmer" of your own!

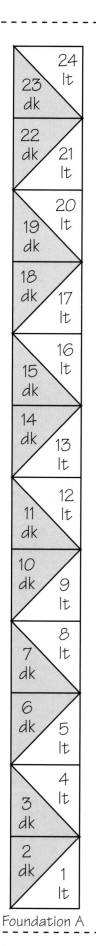

Foundation A

QUILT SIZE: 12" x 13 1/2"
BLOCK SIZE: 3/4" square

MATERIALS

Yardage is estimated for 44" fabric.
• 336 scraps, half light, half dark (all different for a charm quilt) each one at least 2" square
• 1/8 yard fabric for the inner border
• 1/4 yard fabric for the outer border
• 14" x 15 1/2" piece of backing fabric
• 14" x 15 1/2" piece of thin batting
• 1/8 yard binding fabric
• Paper for foundations (optional)

NOTE: *This little quilt is easily foundation pieced. If you wish to use this technique, follow the* Foundation Piecing *instructions in* General Techniques *to make the foundations and to piece the rows. Make 7 foundations from pattern A and 7 from pattern B. Piece the rows as indicated on the foundation patterns. Lay out the rows, alternating row A and row B. Then follow the directions under Assembly beginning with "Join the rows."*

CUTTING FOR TRADITIONAL PIECING

For a scrap quilt (with fabrics repeated):
• Cut 84: 2" squares, light scraps
• Cut 84: 2" squares, dark scraps
For a charm quilt:
• Cut 168: 2" squares, different light scraps
• Cut 168: 2" squares, different dark scraps

PIECING

• Layer one dark 2" square and one light 2" square right sides together. Using a pencil, draw a diagonal line from corner to corner. Stitch 1/4" to the right and left of this line. Cut along the pencil line to yield 2 identical bias squares. Repeat with the remaining 2" squares. NOTE: *If you are making a charm quilt, separate the blocks into 2 piles as you cut them apart. You will use half of the blocks. Save the other half for*

another project.
• Open the bias squares and press the seams toward the dark fabric. Trim the seams to 1/8". Using a bias square ruler, trim the squares to 1 1/4".

ASSEMBLY

• Lay out 12 bias squares and join them to make row A. Press all the seams in the same direction. Trim the seams to 1/8". Make 7 rows.
• Lay out 12 bias squares and join

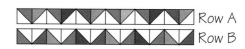

Row A
Row B

them to make row B. Press all the seams in the opposite direction from those in row A. Trim the seams to 1/8". Make 7 rows.
• Lay out the rows alternating row A and row B.
• Join the rows. Press. Trim the seams to 1/8".
• Measure the length of the patchwork. Cut 2 inner borders 1" wide by that length. Sew the borders to the sides of the patchwork.
• Measure the width of the patchwork (including borders). Cut 2 inner borders 1" wide by that width. Sew the borders to the top and bottom of the patchwork.
• Measure the length of the patchwork (including borders). Cut 2 outer borders 1 7/8" wide by that length. Using a 5/8" seam, sew the borders to the sides of the patchwork. Using this large seam allowance makes the piecing more manageable. Check the 1/8" inner border for accuracy. Rip and readjust if necessary. Press the border and trim the seam allowance to 1/8".
• Measure the width of the patchwork (including borders). Cut 2 outer borders 1 7/8" wide by that width. Using a 5/8" seam, sew the borders to

(continued on bottom of page 21)

Foundation B

Country Living

This traditional design gives you a simple field in which to play.

QUILT SIZE: 18 3/4" square
BLOCK SIZE: 4 1/4" square

MATERIALS

Yardage is estimated for 44" fabric.
• 18 dark print scraps (some medium) at least 3" square
• 18 light print scraps (some medium) at least 3" square
• 1/8 yard dark blue print
• 1/3 yard light print fabric for sashing and borders
• 1/8 yard binding fabric
• 21" square of backing fabric
• 21" square of thin batting

CUTTING

• Cut 18: 3" squares from dark or medium scraps
• Cut 18: 3" squares from light or medium scraps
• Cut 18: 1 1/4" x 2 1/4" strips, dark blue print
• Cut 9: 1 1/4" x 4 3/4" strips, same dark blue print
• Cut 6: 1 3/4" x 4 3/4" strips, light print, for the sashing
• Cut 2: 1 3/4" x 15 3/4" strips, light print, for the sashing

PIECING

NOTE: *Substitute some medium prints for several darks and lights to add interest to the quilt.*
• Layer one dark 3" square and one light 3" square right sides together. Using a pencil, draw a diagonal line from corner to corner on the light square. Stitch 1/4" to the right and left of this line. Cut along the pencil line. Open the squares and press the seams toward the dark fabric. Using a bias square ruler, trim the squares to 2 1/4". Make 36.
• Sew a 1 1/4" x 2 1/4" dark blue strip between two pieced squares to make a pieced unit, as shown. Make 18.

• Sew a 1 1/4" x 4 3/4" dark blue strip between two pieced units to complete a block, as shown. Make 9.

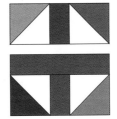

• Sew the blocks in 3 rows of 3, adding the 1 3/4" x 4 3/4" sashing strips between the blocks.
• Sew the rows together, adding the 1 3/4" x 15 3/4" sashing strips between the rows.
• Measure the length of the patchwork. Cut 2 light print borders 2" wide by that length. Sew the borders to opposite sides of the quilt.
• Measure the width of the patchwork (including borders). Cut 2 light print borders 2" wide by that width. Sew the borders to the remaining sides of the quilt.

FINISHING

• Layer the quilt top, batting and backing. Baste. Bind the edges following the instructions in *General Techniques*.

QUILTING

• Quilt a squiggle in the center of each bias square and in the center of the cross. I used the wave border design shown on page 9.

Charmeuse continued

the top and bottom of the patchwork. Check the 1/8" inner border for accuracy. Rip and readjust if necessary. Press the border and trim the seam allowance to 1/8".
• If you used paper foundations, remove them now.

FINISHING

• Layer the quilt top, batting and backing. Baste. Bind the edges following the instructions in *General Techniques*.

QUILTING

• Quilt along the diagonal of each block, making a zigzag design.

Full-Size Border Quilting Design for Charmeuse

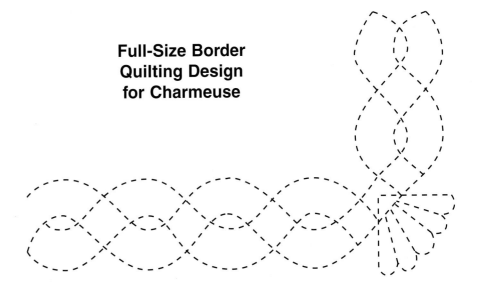

Tumbler Charm

This traditional favorite can be pieced
or stitched on paper foundations.

QUILT SIZE: 13 3/4" x 17"

MATERIALS

Yardage is estimated for 44" fabric. For a charm quilt, use 99 different print scraps.
- 50 light print scraps (some mediums), 2 1/2" square
- 49 dark print scraps (some mediums), 2 1/2" square
- 1/8 yard stripe for the inner border
- 1/4 yard dark print for the outer border
- 1/8 yard binding fabric
- 16" x 19" piece of backing fabric
- 16" x 19" piece of thin batting
- Paper for foundations (optional)

NOTE: *Throughout the quilt, substitute some mediums for several darks and lights to add interest to the quilt. Vary the texture of adjacent prints. Try adding a conversation print or two to add a touch of whimsy and create focal points.*

PIECING

For traditional piecing
- Make templates from the patterns and cut 41 dark A's and 40 light A's. Cut 8 dark B's and 10 light B's.
- Lay out nine A's and two light print B's, beginning with a light print B and alternating lights and darks, as shown.

- Sew the units together to form a row. Press the seam allowances toward the dark fabrics. Make 5.
- Lay out nine A's and two dark print B's, beginning with a dark print B and alternating darks and lights. Sew the units together to form a row. Press the seam allowances toward the dark fabrics. Make 4.
- Follow the directions under ASSEMBLY to complete your quilt top.

For foundation piecing
- *Follow the* Foundation Piecing *instructions in* General Techniques *to make the foundations and to piece the rows. Join the*

foundation patterns by matching the dots to make a continuous row. Make 9 foundations.
For 5 foundations:
- Begin with a light print scrap in position 1. Alternate light and dark scraps.
For 4 foundations:
- Begin with a dark print scrap in position 1. Alternate dark and light scraps.
- Baste each foundation in the seam allowance and trim on the broken line.

ASSEMBLY
- Lay out the rows according to the Assembly Diagram and join the rows.
- Measure the length of the patchwork.

Cut 2 stripe borders 3/4" wide by that length. Sew the borders to the long sides of the patchwork.
- Measure the width of the patchwork (including borders). Cut 2 stripe borders 3/4" wide by that width. Sew the borders to the remaining sides of the patchwork.
- Measure the length of the patchwork (including borders). Cut 2 dark print borders 1 3/4" wide by that length. Sew the borders to the long sides of the patchwork.
- Measure the width of the patchwork (including borders). Cut 2 dark print borders 1 3/4" wide by that width. Sew the

(continued on page 23)

Full-Size Foundation Pattern for Tumbler Charm
Match the dots to make the complete foundation pattern.

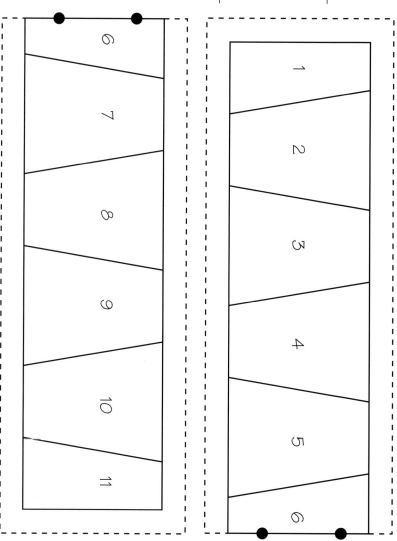

Tumbler Charm continued

borders to the remaining sides of the patchwork.

FINISHING
- Press the quilt top and remove the paper foundations.
- Layer the quilt top, batting and backing. Baste. Bind the edges following the instructions in *General Techniques*.

QUILTING
- Quilt in the ditch with a continuous quilting line.
- I used a simple cable for my border.

Assembly Diagram for Tumbler Charm

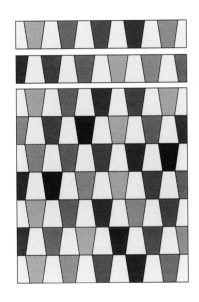

Full-Size Template Patterns for Tumbler Charm

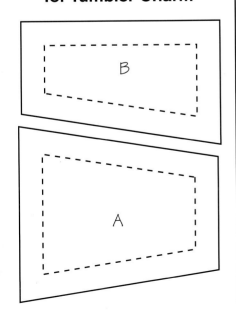

House Medallion

Homespun words of wisdom adorn this cozy little quilt.

QUILT SIZE: 9 3/4" square
BLOCK SIZE: 3 1/2" x 3 3/4"

MATERIALS
Yardage is estimated for 44" fabric.
- 8" square scrap for the house
- 4" square scrap for the roof
- 6" square scrap for the sky
- Scrap of grass fabric at least 2" x 6"
- Assorted scraps including blue, red, purple, brown, green, gold, pink and black (I used mostly darks and mediums with some lights. 60-100 different fabrics will give you the desired variety)
- 1/8 yard muslin or very light fabric with a subtle print for the second border
- 1/8 yard dark print for the third border
- 1/8 yard binding fabric
- 11 3/4" square of backing fabric
- 11 3/4" square of thin batting
- Black or brown fine tip Pigma pen
- Paper for foundations

CUTTING
- Cut 1: A, light scrap, for the gable
- Cut 1: B, dark scrap, for the roof
- Cut 2: 1" x 4 1/4" strips, sky scrap
- Cut 1: 1 1/4" x 5" strip, grass fabric
NOTE: *If you prefer to make your quilt without chimneys, cut the following:*
- Cut 1: 1 1/8" x 4" strip, sky scrap

PIECING
Follow the Foundation Piecing *instructions in* General Techniques *to make the foundations and to piece the blocks. Make 1 foundation each of A, B, C, D, E and F. Make 2 each of G and H.*
For foundation A:
- Use the following fabrics in these positions:
  - 1 - house fabric
  - 2, 3 - one light print
  - 4, 5, 6, 7 - house fabric
  - 8 - medium print
  - 9, 10 - house fabric
  - 11 - Join an A piece and a B piece to

make one unit, then sew it to the house section in position 11.

12, 13 - sky scrap
For foundation B:
NOTE: *If you prefer to make your house without chimneys and have already cut the sky piece, skip this section and go on to foundations C through F.*
- Use the following fabrics in these positions:
  - 1 - sky scrap
  - 2, 3 - brown print
  - 4, 5, 6 - sky scrap
For foundations C through F (the first border):
- Use dark and medium scraps randomly and piece in numerical order.
For 2 foundation G's (the fourth border):
- Use the following fabrics in these positions:
  - 1 - light print
  - 2 - dark print
  - 3, 4, 5 - light prints
  - 6 - dark print
  - 7 - light print
  - 8 to 25 - Continue alternating dark and light print scraps through position 25
  - 26 - light print
  - 27 - dark print
  - 28, 29 - light prints
For 2 foundation H's (the fourth border):
- Start with a light print scrap in position 1 and alternate dark and light print scraps through position 21.
- Baste each foundation in the seam allowance and trim on the broken line.

ASSEMBLY
- Sew foundation A and either foundation B or the 1 1/8" x 4" sky scrap together to make the house unit.
- Sew the 1" x 4 1/4" sky scrap strips to the sides of the house unit.

(continued on page 24)

House Medallion continued

- Sew the 1 1/4" x 5" grass strip to the bottom of the house unit.
- Sew foundation D to the bottom of the house unit.
- Sew foundation C to the top of the house unit.
- Sew foundation E to the right side of the house unit.
- Sew foundation F to the left side of the house unit.
- Measure the length of the patchwork. Cut 2 muslin or light print borders 3/4" wide by that length. Sew the borders to the sides of the patchwork.
- Measure the width of the patchwork (including borders). Cut 2 muslin or light print borders 3/4" wide by the width of the patchwork. Sew the borders to the top and bottom of the patchwork.
- Measure the length of the patchwork (including borders). Cut 2 dark print borders 1" wide by that length. Sew the borders to the sides of the patchwork.
- Measure the width of the patchwork (including borders). Cut 2 dark print borders 1" wide by that width. Sew the borders to the top and bottom of the patchwork.
- Square the patchwork unit to 8".
- Referring to the photo for color placement, sew the H foundations to the top and bottom of the patchwork.
- Sew the G foundations to the sides of the patchwork.
- Press the quilt top and remove the paper foundations.

WRITING
- Choose a four-line verse or quote to frame your patchwork. Cut scrap paper the length of the muslin border and write the words on the paper first to determine proper size and spacing of your lettering. When writing on the quilt itself, lay the paper just above the space you are writing on and use it as a placement guide.

FINISHING
- Layer the quilt top, batting and backing. Baste. Bind the edges following the instructions in *General Techniques*.

QUILTING
- Quilt in the ditch.

ANOTHER IDEA
Choose one of these quotes to write in the border:
- True friends are always together in spirit.

    Turn your ear to the wind, you'll hear it.

    I wish for more hours with you I could spend.

    My friendship with you will never end.
    —old sampler verse

- If there is light in the soul, there will be beauty in the person.

    If there is beauty in the person, there will be harmony in the house.

    If there is harmony in the house, there will be order in the nation.

    If there is order in the nation, there will be peace in the world.
    —Chinese proverb

Full-Size Foundation Patterns for House Medallion

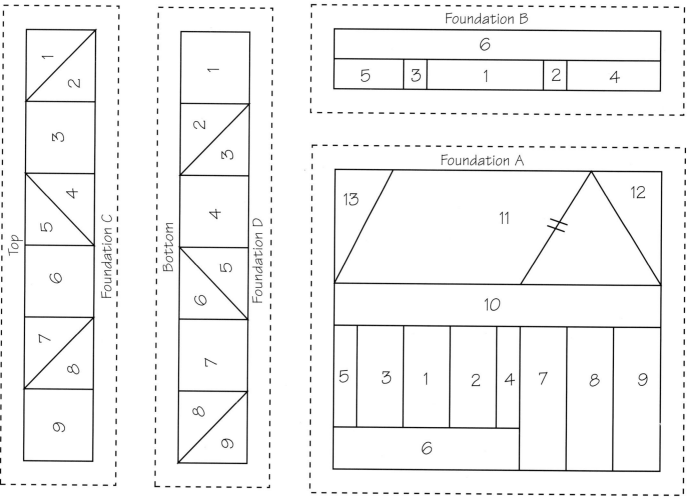

Full-Size Template Patterns for House Medallion

B Roof

A Gable

Full-Size Foundation Patterns for House Medallion

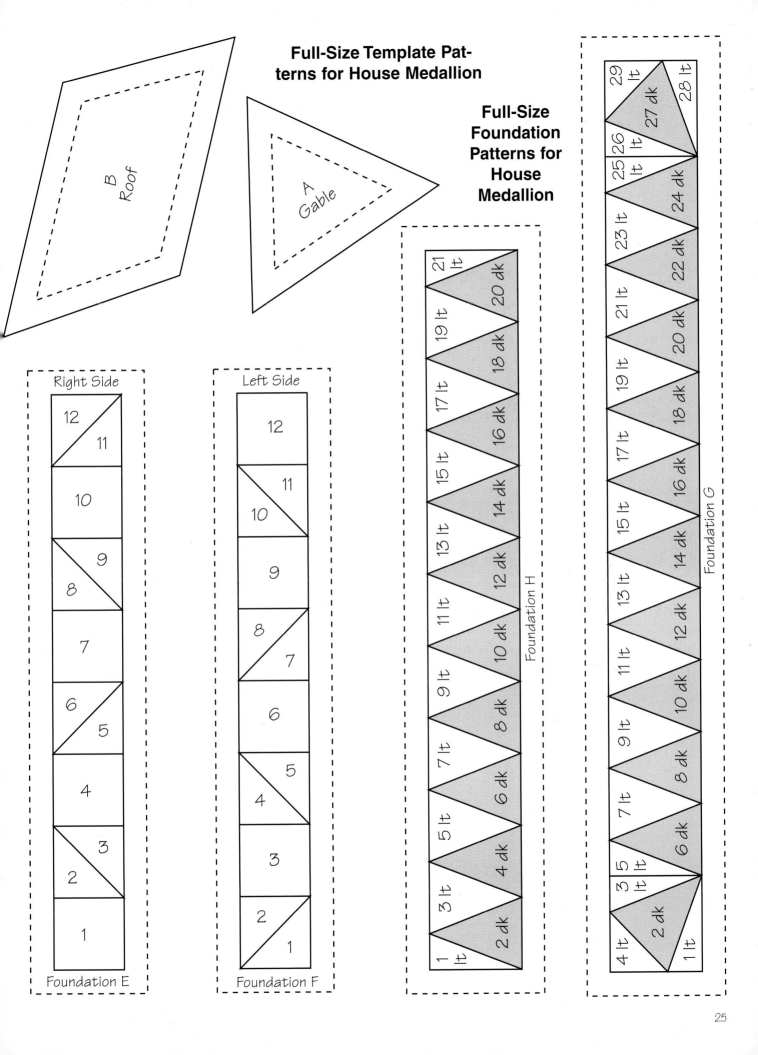

Right Side

| 12 |
| 11 |
| 10 |
| 9 |
| 8 |
| 7 |
| 6 |
| 5 |
| 4 |
| 3 |
| 2 |
| 1 |

Foundation E

Left Side

| 12 |
| 11 |
| 10 |
| 9 |
| 8 |
| 7 |
| 6 |
| 5 |
| 4 |
| 3 |
| 2 |
| 1 |

Foundation F

Foundation H
21 lt, 20 dk, 19 lt, 18 dk, 17 lt, 16 dk, 15 lt, 14 dk, 13 lt, 12 dk, 11 lt, 10 dk, 9 lt, 8 dk, 7 lt, 6 dk, 5 lt, 4 dk, 3 lt, 2 dk, 1 lt

Foundation G
29 lt, 28 lt, 27 dk, 26 lt, 25 lt, 24 dk, 23 lt, 22 dk, 21 lt, 20 dk, 19 lt, 18 dk, 17 lt, 16 dk, 15 lt, 14 dk, 13 lt, 12 dk, 11 lt, 10 dk, 9 lt, 8 dk, 7 lt, 6 dk, 5 lt, 4 lt, 3 lt, 2 dk, 1 lt

Button Up

Showcase your favorite buttons on a fun background!

QUILT SIZE: 15" square
BLOCK SIZE: 1 1/2" square

MATERIALS
Yardage is estimated for 44" fabric.
• Assorted light, medium and dark print and plaid scraps totaling 1/2 yard
• Red scraps for the zigzag border totaling 1/4 yard
• 1/4 yard gold print for the border
• 1/8 yard binding fabric
• 17" square of backing fabric
• 17" square of batting
• Approximately 105 buttons; I used 3/8" buttons
• Paper for foundations (optional)

CUTTING
For 25 Four Patch blocks:
• Cut 50: 1 1/4" squares, dark scraps
• Cut 50: 1 1/4" squares, light scraps
If you choose to piece the zigzag borders traditionally:
• Cut 62: 1 5/8" squares, red scraps
• Cut 62: 1 5/8" squares, gold
• Cut 4: 1 1/4" squares, gold

PIECING
• Join one light 1 1/4" square and one dark 1 1/4" square to make a pieced rectangle. Press the seam allowance toward the dark square. Make 2.
• Join the pieced rectangles to make a Four Patch block. Make 25.
• *Follow the* Foundation Piecing *instructions in* General Techniques *to make 24 Square-within-a-Square foundations and to piece the blocks.*

• Use the following fabrics in these positions:
    1 - dark scrap
    2, 3, 4, 5 - one light print

ASSEMBLY
• Alternating Four-Patch blocks and Square-within-a-Square blocks, lay out 7 rows of 7 blocks. Sew the blocks into rows.
• Press the seams of adjacent rows in opposite directions. Join the rows.

ZIGZAG BORDER
For foundation pieced borders:
Follow the Foundation Piecing *instructions in* General Techniques *to make the foundations and to piece the rows. Join the foundation patterns by matching the dots to make a continuous row. Make 4 foundations from each border row pattern and 4 from each corner row pattern.*
For border row A:
• Use the following fabrics in these positions:
    1 - red scrap
    2, 3 - gold
    4, 5 - red scraps
    6, 7 - gold
    8, 9 - red scraps
Continue with the established pattern to make a row of 28 triangles.
For border row B:
• Use the following fabrics in these positions:
    1 - gold
    2, 3 - red scraps
    4, 5 - gold

6, 7 - red scraps
8, 9 - gold
Continue with the established pattern to make a row of 28 triangles.
For corner row A:
• Use the following fabrics in these positions:
    1 - red scrap
    2 - gold
    3 - red scrap
    4 - gold
For corner row B:
• Use the following fabrics in these positions:
    1 - gold
    2 - red scrap
    3 - gold
• Baste each foundation in the seam allowance and trim on the broken line.
• Sew a border row A and a border row B together along their length to make a zigzag border, as shown. Make 4.

• Sew a corner row A and a corner row B together to make a corner block, as shown. Make 4.

For traditional pieced borders:
• Using a pencil and a ruler, draw a diagonal line from corner to corner on the wrong side of the 1 5/8" gold squares.
• Place a gold square and a red square right sides together and sew 1/4" on each

Full-Size Foundation Patterns for Button Up

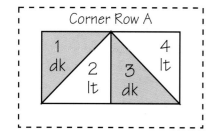

Corner Row A

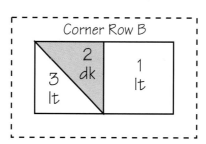

Corner Row B

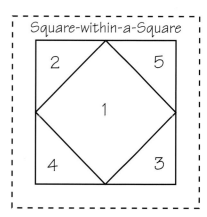

Square-within-a-Square

ide of the line. Make 62. Cut each sewn quare on the drawn line to yield 124 bias squares.

• Sew 4 bias squares together o make a chevron unit, as hown. Make 28.
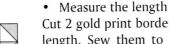

• Sew 7 chevron units in a row to make a zigzag border. Make 4.

• Sew 3 bias squares and a 1/4" gold square together to make a corner block. Make 4.

ASSEMBLY

• Sew 2 zigzag borders to opposite sides of the quilt.

• Sew a corner block to each end of the

remaining zigzag borders, as shown.

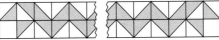

• Sew these borders to the remaining sides of the quilt.

• Measure the length of the patchwork. Cut 2 gold print borders, 1" wide by that length. Sew them to opposite sides of the patchwork.

• Measure the width of the patchwork (including borders). Cut 2 gold print borders, 1" wide by that width. Sew them to the remaining sides of the patchwork.

• Press the quilt top and remove the paper foundations.

FINISHING

• Layer the quilt top, batting and backing. Baste. Bind the edges following the instructions in *General Techniques*.

QUILTING

• Quilt the blocks in the ditch. Quilt an X over the light squares in the Four Patch blocks.

• Quilt border zigzag in the ditch. Add an additional scalloped line of quilting, if desired.

• Sew buttons to the quilt top, barely piercing the backing of your quilt.

Full-Size Foundation Patterns for Button Up

Match the dots to make the complete foundation pattern.

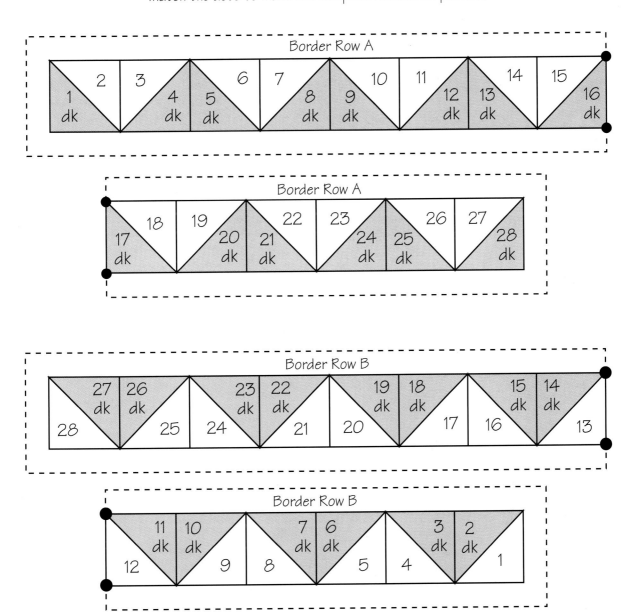

Sweethearts

This tiny quilt is so impressive your friends will be shaking their heads!

QUILT SIZE: 3 3/4" x 4 1/4"
BLOCK SIZE: 5/8" x 7/8"

MATERIALS
- 6" square of muslin
- 1" squares of 9 dark or medium scraps
- 4" x 8" dark scrap for border
- 3" x 10" scrap for the binding
- 5 1/2" x 6 1/2" piece of backing fabric
- 5 1/2" x 6 1/2" piece of thin batting
- Paper backed fusible web (such as Wonder-Under™ or Heat 'n Bond®)

CUTTING
- Cut 9: 1 1/8" x 1 3/8" rectangles, muslin
- Cut 1: 1 1/8" x 14" strip, red stripe, for the border

DIRECTIONS
- Lay out the rectangles, with the long sides placed vertically, in 3 rows of 3.
- Stitch the rectangles into rows, press the seams of adjacent rows in opposite directions. Join the rows.
- Measure the width of the patchwork.

Cut 2 borders 1 1/8" wide by that width. Sew the borders to the top and bottom of the quilt.
- Measure the length of the patchwork (including borders). Cut 2 borders 1 1/8" wide by that length. Sew the borders to the sides of the quilt.
- Make a template for the heart.
- Draw a grid of 3/4" squares 3 rows across and 3 rows down on the smooth side of the fusible web. Center and trace the heart template in each square. Cut the squares apart on the drawn lines.
- Fuse a square to the wrong side of each 1" square scrap. Cut out the hearts.
- Fuse a heart to the center of each muslin rectangle.
- Using matching thread, whipstitch around the edge of each heart. This gives the illusion of hand appliqué. No one will ever guess you didn't turn those edges under!

FINISHING
- Layer the quilt top, batting and back-

ing. There is no need to baste a quilt this small. Bind the edges following the instructions in *General Techniques*.

QUILTING
- Quilt around each heart. This gives the hearts depth and furthers the illusion of hand appliqué. Quilt in the ditch around the muslin blocks, if desired.

ANOTHER IDEA
Back your tiny quilt in plain muslin and use a Pigma pen to write a message or quote to the lucky recipient.
- "A friend loveth at all times." Proverbs 17:17
- "Home is where the heart is."
- "Your heart's desires be with you." William Shakespeare
- "Delight thyself in the Lord and He will give you the desires of your heart." Psalm 37:4
- "He that is of a merry heart hath a continual feast." Proverbs 15:15

Puss in the Corner

A motif in the center of each tiny block adds whimsy!

QUILT SIZE: 6" square
BLOCK SIZE: 1" square

MATERIALS
- Assorted dark and light print scraps (I used vintage fabrics.)
- 13 light print scraps, each at least 1 1/2" x 4 1/2"
- 6" square dark scrap for the border
- 4" x 7" scrap for the binding
- 8" square of backing fabric
- 8" square of thin batting

CUTTING
- Cut 13: 1" squares, dark prints, for the block centers
- Cut 53: 3/4" squares, dark and light

prints, for the block corners
- Cut 4: 3/4" x 1" strips from each of the 13 light prints
- Cut 12: 1 1/2" squares, light prints, for the alternate blocks

PIECING
- Sew a 3/4" x 1" light strip between two 3/4" squares to make a pieced strip, as shown. Make 26 (2 from each of the 13 light prints).
- Press the seam allowances toward the squares and trim them to 1/8".
- Lay out 2 pieced strips, a 1" dark square and two 3/4" x 1" light strips, as shown. NOTE: *The 3/4" x 1" light strips*

match within the blocks. Stitch the units into rows and join the rows to complete a block. Trim the seam allowances to 1/8" as you go. Make 13 blocks.

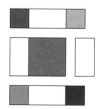

ASSEMBLY
- Referring to the photo as needed, lay out 3 pieced blocks and two 1 1/2" light print squares. Join the units to form a row. Make 3.

(continued on bottom of page 29)

Pineapple Log Cabin Color Study

Play with color in this simple pattern. You'll be delighted with the results!

QUILT SIZE: 11" square
BLOCK SIZE: 2 1/2" square

MATERIALS

Yardage is estimated for 44" fabric.
- 9 scraps of red print at least 1 1/4" square each
- 18 scraps of tan, beige or other neutral at least 1 1/4" x 1 3/4" each
- 9 scraps of navy at least 3/4" x 1 1/2" each
- 9 scraps of pink at least 3/4" x 1 1/2" each
- 9 scraps of brown at least 3/4" x 1 3/4" each
- 1/8 yard blue for the inner border
- 1/8 yard brown check for the outer border
- 1/8 yard binding fabric
- 13" square of backing fabric
- 13" square of thin batting
- Paper for foundations

CUTTING
- Cut 2: 1" x 8" strips, blue, for the inner border
- Cut 2: 1" x 9" strips, blue, for the inner border
- Cut 2: 1 1/2" x 9" strips, brown check, for the outer border
- Cut 2: 1 1/2" x 11" strips, brown check, for the outer border

PIECING
- *Follow the* Foundation Piecing *instructions in* General Techniques *to make 9 foundations and to piece the blocks.* NOTE: *Each block has the same color (but different fabric) in the same location.*
- Use the following fabrics in these positions:
  - 1 - red
  - 2, 3, 4, 5 - tan, beige or other neutral
  - 6, 7, 8, 9 - navy
  - 10, 11, 12, 13 - pink
  - 14, 15, 16, 17 - brown
  - 18, 19, 20, 21 - tan, beige or other neutral
- Baste each block in the seam allowance and trim on the broken line.

ASSEMBLY
- Lay out 3 rows of 3 blocks.
- Sew the blocks together in rows. Press the seams of adjacent rows in opposite directions. Join the rows.
- Sew the 1" x 8" blue strips to opposite sides of the quilt.
- Sew the 1" x 9" blue strips to the remaining sides of the quilt.
- Sew the 1 1/2" x 9" brown check strips to opposite sides of the quilt.
- Sew the 1 1/2" x 11" brown check strips to the remaining sides of the quilt.
- Press the quilt top and remove the paper foundations.

FINISHING
- Layer the quilt top, batting and backing. Baste. Bind the edges following the instructions in *General Techniques*.

QUILTING
- Quilt in the ditch.

Puss in the Corner continued

- Lay out three 1 1/2" light print squares and 2 pieced blocks. Join the units to form a row. Make 2.
- Press the seams of adjacent rows in opposite directions. Join the rows.
- Measure the length of the patchwork. Cut 2 dark scrap borders 1 1/8" wide by that length. Sew the borders to opposite sides of the patchwork.
- Measure the width of the patchwork (including borders). Cut 2 dark scrap borders 1 1/8" wide by that width. Sew the borders to the remaining sides of the patchwork.

FINISHING
- Layer the quilt top, batting and backing. If you used vintage fabric, baste carefully—it tends to be brittle.
- Cut 4 binding strips each 5/8" wide and bind the edges following the instructions in *General Techniques*.

QUILTING
- Quilt around the center square of each pieced block. Quilt an "X" across each alternate block. Quilt along the border where it meets the patchwork.

Full-Size Foundation Pattern for Pineapple Log Cabin Color Study

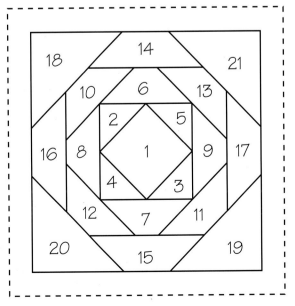

Teacups

Put the kettle on to boil and
pick out your favorite fabrics!

QUILT SIZE: 13" x 13 5/8"
BLOCK SIZES: 2" x 1 5/8" and 2 1/2" x 1 5/8"

MATERIALS

Yardage is estimated for 44" fabric.
• 20 dark or medium print scraps at least 3" square
• 1/4 yard muslin or light solid
• 1/4 yard check for "shelves" and inner border
• 3" x 11" strip of check or stripe fabric for the narrow accent border
• 1/8 yard gold for the outer border
• 15" x 17 1/2" piece of backing fabric
• 15" x 17 1/2" piece of thin batting
• 1/8 yard binding fabric
• Paper for foundations

CUTTING

• Cut 4: 3/4" x 9" strips, check, for the shelves
• Cut 2: 1" x 9" strips, check, for the inner border
• Cut 2: 1" x 10 5/8" strips, check, for the inner border

PIECING

Follow the Foundation Piecing *instructions in* General Techniques *to make the foundations and to piece the blocks. Make 15 foundations from pattern A and 5 from pattern B.*
For foundation A:
• Use the following fabrics in these positions:

1 - muslin
2, 3, 4 - one dark or medium print
5 - muslin
6 - dark or medium print
7, 8 - muslin
For Foundation B:
• Use the following fabrics in these positions:

1 - muslin
2, 3, 4 - one dark or medium print
5 - muslin
6 - dark or medium print
7, 8, 9 - muslin
• Baste each foundation in the seam allowance and trim on the broken line.

ASSEMBLY

• Lay out 3 "A" blocks and 1 "B" block, placing the "B" block at the right end of the row. Join the blocks to form a row. Make 5 rows.
• Sew a 3/4" x 9" check strip between each row.
• Sew the 1" x 9" check strips to the top and bottom of the quilt.
• Sew the 1" x 10 5/8" check strips to the sides of the quilt.
• Measure the width of the patchwork. Cut 2 check or stripe borders 3/4" wide by that width. Sew the borders to the top and bottom of the patchwork.
• Measure the length of the patchwork (including borders). Cut 2 check or stripe borders 3/4" wide by that length. Sew the

borders to the sides of the patchwork.
• Measure the width of the patchwork (including borders). Cut 2 gold borders 1 3/4" wide by that width. Sew the borders to the top and bottom of the patchwork.
• Measure the length of the patchwork (including borders). Cut 2 gold borders 1 3/4" wide by that length. Sew the borders to the sides of the patchwork.
• Press the quilt top and remove the paper foundations.

FINISHING

• Layer the quilt top, batting and backing. Baste. Bind the edges following the instructions in *General Techniques*.

QUILTING

• Quilt in the ditch around the cups. Quilt lines to illustrate steam rising from some of the cups.
• Draw freehand steam in the border. Camouflage a message in curly writing interspersed with the curls of steam.

OTHER IDEAS

• Quilt a quote into the border. "Love and scandal are the best sweeteners of tea." Henry Fielding
• Piece four teacups and make a coaster.

Full-Size Foundation Patterns for Teacups

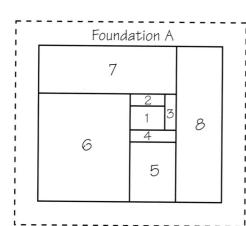

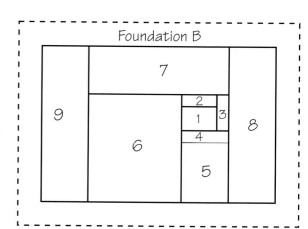

Star Struck

Pick one interesting fabric for a star quality mini!

QUILT SIZE: 16" x 19 3/4"
BLOCK SIZE: 3" square

MATERIALS
Yardage is estimated for 44" fabric.
- Assorted dark scraps totaling 1/2 yard
- Assorted light scraps totaling 1/4 yard
- Small piece of a unique conversation print (I used celebrity face fabric.)
- 1/2 yard light sashing fabric
- 1/4 yard blue border fabric
- 4 red print scraps, each at least 2 1/4" square
- 1/8 yard binding fabric—I used gold
- 18" x 22" piece of backing fabric
- 18" x 22" piece of thin batting

CUTTING
For each block:
- Cut 3: 1 1/4" squares, dark fabric
- Cut 1: 1 1/4" square, conversation print, centering the motif
- Cut 4: 1 1/4" squares, light fabric
Also:
- Cut 48: 2" squares, dark scraps
- Cut 48: 2" squares, light scraps
- Cut 31: 1 1/4" x 3 1/2" strips, sashing fabric
- Cut 20: 1 1/4" corner squares, sashing fabric
- Cut 4: 2 1/4" squares, red print

PIECING
- Assemble three 1 1/4" dark squares and a 1 1/4" conversation print square into a Four Patch unit. Make 12.
- Layer a dark and a light 2" square, right sides together. On the wrong side of the light fabric, draw a diagonal line, corner to corner. Stitch 1/4" to the right

and the left of the line. Make 48.
- Cut each square along the drawn line. You will have 96 pieced squares. Press the seams toward the dark fabric. Using a bias square ruler, trim the squares to 1 1/4".
- Sew 2 pieced squares together to make a pieced rectangle. Make 48.

- Lay out a pieced rectangle and two 1 1/4" light squares. Stitch them together to form a pieced strip, as shown. Make 24.

- Lay out 2 pieced strips, 2 pieced rectangles and a Four Patch unit. Join them to complete a block, as shown. Make 12.

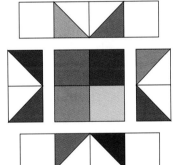

ASSEMBLY
- Choose 3 blocks for row 1. Sew two 1 1/4" x 3 1/2" sashing strips between the blocks and one on each end of the row. Make 4 rows.
- Construct the horizontal sashing by alternating four 1 1/4" corner squares and 3 sashing strips, beginning and end-

ing with a corner square. Make 5. Sew these sashing rows between the rows of blocks and to the top and bottom of the patchwork.
- Measure the width of the patchwork. Cut 2 blue borders 2 1/4" wide by that width plus 1/2". Sew a 2 1/4" red print square to each end of these borders.
- Measure the length of the patchwork. Cut 2 blue borders 2 1/4" wide by that length. Sew the borders to the sides of the patchwork.
- Sew the borders with corner squares to the top and bottom of the quilt.

FINISHING
- Layer the quilt top, batting and backing. Baste. Bind the edges following the instructions in *General Techniques*.

QUILTING
- Quilt in the ditch. A simple wave adorns the border.

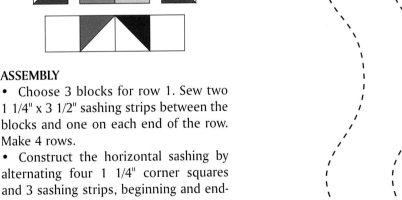

**Full-Size
Border
Quilting
Design for
Starstruck**

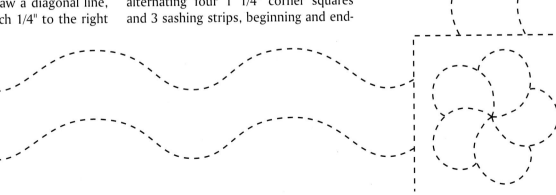

My Favorite Things

We all have our favorites—celebrate yours!

QUILT SIZE: 4 3/4" square
BLOCK SIZE: 1/2" square

MATERIALS
• 36 assorted print scraps at least 1" square—use conversation prints with motifs smaller than 1/2" if desired
• 3" x 12" strip of dark fabric for the border
• 5" x 6" scrap for the binding
• 6" square of backing fabric
• 6" square of thin batting
• Paper for foundations (optional)

NOTE: *If you prefer to piece on foundations, follow the instructions for* Foundation Piecing *in* General Techniques *to make 6 foundations and to piece the rows. Foundation piece adjacent rows from opposite directions. Seams will butt securely when the rows are joined.*

CUTTING
• Cut 36: 1" squares, assorted prints and conversation motifs

• Cut 2: 1 1/8" x 3 1/2" strips, dark print, for the border
• Cut 2: 1 1/8" x 4 3/4" strips, dark print, for the border

PIECING
• Sew six 1" squares into a row. Press the seams in one direction. Trim the seams to 1/8".
• Sew 5 more rows, pressing the seams of adjacent rows in opposite directions. Trim the seams to 1/8".
• Join the rows. Press. Trim the seams.
• Sew the 1 1/8" x 3 1/2" border strips to opposite sides of the of the patchwork.

• Sew the 1 1/8" x 4 3/4" border strips to the remaining sides of the patchwork.

FINISHING
• Layer the quilt top, batting and backing. Baste. Bind the edges following the instructions in *General Techniques.*

QUILTING
• Quilt every other block across the diagonal. To prevent your quilting stitch from distorting the tiny motif, do not quilt across the motif. Quilt up to the motif, run the needle inside the batting to the other side of the motif, and continue quilting.

Full-Size Foundation Pattern for My Favorite Things

1	2	3	4	5	6

Full-Size Cable Border Quilting Design for Hole in the Barn Door

Full-Size Ice Cream Cone Border Quilting Design for Brick Wall Charm